Carola Heine

FAIRYTALE
FOCACCIA

Recipes, some
Inspiration and
Focaccia Art

www.planet-alltag.de/english

Hi fellow bakers and focaccia fans,

please think of this book as written in a clumsy German accent. English is not my native tongue, nor am I entitled by heritage to make Italian food - but my wish to share these delicious recipes with you is quite international. That's why I decided to give you this book about my favorite bread anyway, just as focaccia can be made by everyone: The focaccia is a queen among the many delicious ways to bake a bread in a quick and uncomplicated way.

Even before I got to know this Italian flat bread so much better, I liked to welcome my guests with the smell of freshly baked focacce. Cut into strips with olive oil on top, sprinkled with coarse salt – roasted briefly in the oven, crisp and smelling deliciously. Even the purchased kind of focaccia is a great appetizer or side dish. When I learned that I can serve freshly baked focaccia in no time at all, I wanted to know how the real traditional focacce in Italy are made. One recipe idea led to another and to more. The recipes in this booklet will help to make your Fairytale Focaccia the highlight of every buffet. With delicious toppings or spices kneaded into the dough and fillings, this bread is also a full meal. Children will love to decorate the dough.

Focaccia with a topping looks even prettier. I was thrilled, when I saw a wonderful Focaccia Gardenscape by baker Teri Culletto in spring 2020 (Instagram @vineyardbaker). According to nytimes.com, she posted the first Focaccia Garden on Instagram, starting the trend of putting colorful vegetables on flat bread in order to *bakepaint* a picture. These pretty breadscapes are called Flower Focaccia, Focaccia Garden or **Gardenscape Focaccia**. They are now made everywhere in the world and put proudly on display online especially in social media and blogs..

Hence the idea for this book about focacce and Focaccia Art and the beautiful coloured Fairytale Focaccia. Enjoy your baking, guten Appetit and buon appetito!

Carola Heine
www.planet-alltag.de/english

We baked and photographed every recipe in
this book ourselves (several times) when we
ate our way through "Fairytale Focaccia".

Perfect Focaccia ...

... has a crispy, slightly golden crust. It's soft and fluffy inside, with large air holes and pores.

Literally everything can make a difference, when you follow a recipe to bake a bread: The oven, the flour, the state of the yeast, the room temperature, the cooking time in the oven or the type of oil. Baking experience shows that lots of factors influence how flat, high, wet or dense a bread turns out - every single time.

Fairytale Focaccia ...

... can even be made with any dough that has become a little too soft or firm. Just put the vegetables on top.

The one thing you should pay attention to: Once the dough has risen, it is not kneaded again or any further. Please keep some notes on the type of flour you used and the temperature of your oven plus the timing - just to ensure you can reliably repeat every successful result.

Table of contents

Let's start our visit to the land of focaccia with basic recipes for everyday life, followed by fancy party recipes for guests and finally our fabulous colourful »Fairytale Focaccia«.

Page   Content

Tips for Fabulous Focaccia:

Preheat your oven to 430°F (220°C) to bake a focaccia with gardenscape or other toppings. Bake the bread for a maximum of **20–25 minutes** until the outer crust turns golden brown.

You will achieve the best result with pizza flour (Type OO), but any kind of flour will do. Always use a high quality **virgin olive oil** and some good **coarse salt** in and on the dough.

For the perfect crispness use some **durum wheat semolina** in the dough, underneath when kneading or on the slightly oiled baking tray to prevent sticking and add more crust.

Classic Focaccia Recipe for every day

The classic focaccia can easily be integrated into any schedule: Only one hour for the dough to rise plus a baking time of 20 to 25 minutes at 430°F (220°C) for a bread with toppings to 480°F (250°C) degrees for bread with salt and oil only.

4 SERVINGS AS MAIN COURSE
6-8 SERVINGS AS SIDE DISH OR STARTER

PREPARATION TIME CIRCA 100 MINUTES WITH
1 HOUR OF DOUGH REST 20-25 MINUTES BAKING TIME

Ingredients:
4 Cups (500 g) flour
42 g (1 cube) fresh yeast
300 milliliter lukewarm water
1 teaspoon sugar
1 teaspoon kitchen salt
2 tablespoons virgin olive oil in the dough

On top of the bread, before baking:
4 to 6 tablespoons virgin olive oil
a few pinches of coarse salt
fresh rosmary

If you can't get hold of fresh yeast, you can also use 15 grams of dry yeast.
Take dried rosemary if you can't get fresh spices or try fresh thyme, sage or every other fresh garden herb to put on the focaccia.

Take the bowl of the food processor or one of a similar size to dissolve yeast and sugar in the lukewarm water.

Briefly mix flour and salt and add it to the water. Put 2 tablespoons of virgin oil in and knead thoroughly.

The dough starts out very soft and sticky but will turn into a smooth ball after five to ten minutes of kneading - softer than typical pizza dough.

Split the dough to form 2 to 4 flat focacce, put on a baking tray and leave to rise in a warm place for an hour.

Preheat the oven. Now take your fingertips to put the typical focaccia dents into the flatbread.

Sprinkle with olive oil and coarse salt, put the fresh rosemary on top and bake.

TIP:
ONCE THE DOUGH HAS RISEN, PLEASE DON'T KNEAD IT AGAIN. IT IS ONLY FORMED BY GENTLY PULLING APART AND MAKING LAYERS ON TOP OF EACH OTHER AND FOLDING THEM, NOT BY KNEADING.

Traditional Focaccia

The traditional focaccia requires the dough to be allowed to rise and rest again several times - it will develop its character and aroma this way. The resting period in the fridge can vary from 8–24 hours, which allows for flexible planning.

2 LARGE OR 4 SMALL FOCACCE
EACH 4-6 SERVINGS AS STARTER OR SIDE DISH

PREPARATION TIME: ONE AND A HALF DAYS PLUS
20-25 MINUTES BAKING AT 430-480°F (220-250°C)

The dough has several more opportunities to rise and develop its flavor compared to the faster versions. That's the reason you need less yeast, but you also need a fridge to let it rest overnight.

Ingredients:

4 cups (500 g) pizza flour or flour
(high gluten, all-purpose or bread flour)

5 g dry yeast or 15 g fresh yeast
300-400 ml water
30 ml virgin olive oil for the dough
2 tablespoons olive oil on each focaccia
20 g salt
coarse salt to sprinkle on top
fresh rosemary
(alternatively: thyme or oregano)

Take a large bowl to dissolve the yeast in the water with the help of a wooden spoon. Add oil and salt and finally the flour. Knead everything thoroughly, until the dough comes together.

Leave the bale of dough in the bowl, cover with a piece of cloth and leave to rise in a warm place for an hour (like inside an oven). Loosely pull the dough apart and fold it back together several times. Make one big ball of dough.

Brush the insides of a big bowl with a lid with some olive oil. Put the dough inside, close the lid and put it into the fridge overnight (but at least for 8 hours).

Before baking, the dough is divided into 2 to 4 parts. They are left to rise at room temperature for another hour. Make fingertip dents into the dough, put oil and salt and herbs on top and bake.

TIP:
FOR BEST RESULTS DIVIDE THE BAKING TIME: PUT THE BREAD ON THE LOWER LEVEL OF THE OVEN FOR THE FIRST 10 MINUTES TO MAKE A PERFECT BUTTOM, THEN MOVE UP TO THE MIDDLE GRILL.

Quick Focaccia without yeast

No time and no yeast? No problem: This very fast and easy focaccia recipe with baking powder requires no resting period for the dough and can be made into a nicely decorated flatbread with every kind of topping. We recommend olives.

1 MEDIUM-SIZED FOCACCIA
4-6 SERVINGS AS SIDE DISH OR STARTER

PREPARATION TIME CIRCA 10 MINUTES:
NO DOUGH REST, ONLY 20–25 MINUTES BAKING TIME

Ingredients:

1 and 3/4 cup (200 g) flour
50 g durum wheat semolina
10 g baking powder
5 g salt
250 milliliter water
1 tablespoon virgin olive oil in the dough

2 tablespoons olive oil to put on top
10 g coarse sea-salt
fresh rosemary or other herbs
or vegetable toppings

All those nice recipes for ciabatta, pizza or focaccia profit from a little durum wheat semolina. We also bake with the soft kind of semolina, with bulgur or polenta. The focaccia doesn't mind.

Brush your baking tray with olive oil and sprinkle some semolina on top of the oil. Preheat the Oven to 430°F (220°C).

Take a large bowl to mix flour, baking powder and salt. Add water and a generous tablespoon of virgin olive oil, mix with a wooden spoon.

Sprinkle some semolina on a wooden board and place the mix on top to knead it until it can be made into a smooth lump of dough.

Put it on the baking tray and shape it into a round or square flatbread. Make the typical focaccia dents with your fingertips.

Brush your focaccia with olive oil, sprinkle with salt and rosemary and bake in the preheated oven for 20 to 25 minutes until golden brown.

TIP:
IT DEPENDS ON MANY FACTORS WHETHER A FOCACCIA TURNS OUT AS EXPECTED: FLOUR, FRESHNESS OF INGREDIENTS (YEAST ESPECIALLY), TEMPERATURES AND KNEADING TIME. BUT DON'T WORRY, EVEN THE FLATTEST OF FOCACCE TASTE WELL.

Whole-Wheat Focaccia Bread

Spicy and hearty focacce are really nice in the wholemeal variety. The bread will never be as fluffy and will rarely have the coarse pores of the typical focaccia, but still tastes delicious and is very filling.

4 SERVINGS AS MAIN COURSE
6-8 SERVINGS AS SIDE DISH OR STARTER

PREPARATION TIME CIRCA 360 MINUTES:
REPEATED REST PLUS 20–25 MINUTES BAKING TIME

Ingredients:

21 g fresh yeast or 7 g dry yeast
1 tablespoon sugar
300 ml lukewarm water
4 cups (480 g) spelt or whole-wheat flour
3 tablespoons cornstarch
1 teaspoon salt
3 tablespoons virgin olive oil for the dough
2–3 tablespoons olive oil for the top
coarse sea-salt
herbs, for example rosemary

Whole-Wheat Focaccia might not be so fluffy, but on the other hand you can put pickled vegetables on top, such as antipasti, grilled peppers from a jar or marinated peperoni, olives. Try to combine a topping and a filling.

Take a large bowl and mix yeast and sugar to dissolve in the water. Leave it for 15 minutes.

Mix flour, starch, salt and 3 tablespoons of oil. Add the yeast-water and now stir briefly but vigorously with a wooden spoon, until you have formed a sticky dough ball.

Cover the bowl with a cloth and let it rest for half an hour.

Carefully pull the dough apart and fold it back on top of itself without kneading again. Cover it once more and leave it alone until the dough has doubled in volume (that should take 90 minutes).

Place in a bowl with a lid and put in the refrigerator overnight (or for up to 24 hours).

Before baking, divide and make loosely formed smooth lumps of dough on the oiled baking tray. Leave to rise again for another hour.

Preheat the Oven to 430°F (220°C) and bake for 25–30 minutes.

Potato Focaccia, also with sweet potato or hokkaido pumpkin

We made this variation of focaccia with raw grated potatoes, with baked sweet potatoes and because it was great, also with blanched hokkaido pumpkin. Potato Focaccia has turned out as a delicious eyecatcher every time.

2 FLATBREADS OR 4 SERVINGS AS MAIN COURSE
8 SERVINGS SLICED UP AS SIDE-DISH OR STARTER

PREPARATION TIME CIRCA 100 MINUTES:
60 MINUTES DOUGH REST, 20–25 MINUTES BAKING
TIME

Ingredients:

10 g fresh yeast
500 g waxy potatoes
(300 of which will be used grated raw)
2,5 cups (350 g) wheat flour
coarse salt, 3 tablespoons olive oil
1 tablespoon chopped fresh parsley
200 ml lukewarm water

200 g pickled sun dried tomatoes
in fine stripes
some spoonfuls of oil from the tomatoes
4 cups (400 g) onion slices fried in oil

Peel the potatoes and put 200 grams in cold water for later. Grate the rest coarsely.

Drain the sun-dried tomatoes and keep the oil. Mix the chopped parsley and the salt with three tablespoons of the oil.

Add flour, crumbled yeast and grated potatoes. Knead everything until it comes together as a smooth dough. Cover with a cloth and leave to rise in a warm place for 60 minutes.

Slice the onions into rings and fry them. Set aside. Preheat the oven to 390°F (200°C). Put oil on the baking tray, make 2 flat breads on the tray.

Take the potatoes out of the water and cut them in 3 mm thick slices. Spread the slices, the onion rings and sun-dried tomato stripes evenly on top.

Bake for 40 to 45 minutes. Sprinkle with coarse salt and serve fresh and warm.

Focaccia with Semolina Dough

Quick recipe for fluffy thick mini pizza, focacce and nicely decorated surfaces with patterns and weaves made of dough. This soft and delicious focaccia bread is best served with toppings, spices and herbs can be kneaded into the dough.

4 SMALL BUT HIGH FOCACCIA BREADS
DIAMETER CIRCA 8-9 INCH (20 – 22 CM)

PREPARATION TIME 2 HOURS INCLUDING
1 HOUR TO RISE PLUS 25–30 MINUTES BAKING TIME

Ingredients:

0,5 cup (100 g) durum wheat semolina
400 ml boiling water
(mix and let swell and cool)

4 cups (500 g) bread flour
2 teaspoons sugar
15 g dried yeast (or 42 g fresh, 1 cube)
30 ml virgin olive oil in the dough
1 tablespoon of salt

for each flatbread 1-2 tabelspoons of
olive oil to brush on top
coarse salt, toppings and spices

TIP:
INSTEAD OF DURUM WHEAT SEMOLINA YOU CAN
ALSO USE THE SOFT KIND OF SEMOLINA, POLENTA OR
BULGUR. THE BREAD WILL BE A LITTLE DIFFERENT, BUT
STILL DELICIOUS.

Take a large flat bowl and pour the boiling water on top of the semolina. Mix thoroughly and let it cool down entirely.

Afterwards you can chuck all ingredients into the foodprocessor in kneading mode and mix them together into a smooth dough. No additional water is required. Even if the dough looks crumbly at first, it will come around just fine.

Oil a baking tray and sprinkle with semolina. Make several flat breads and let them rise for 60 minutes covered with a cloth.

Bake at 430°F (220°C) for 25 minutes.

The semolina dough likes toppings and patterns. Cut out hearts or stripes or make a weave and put it back on top. It will become a delicious crust.

Focaccia Cake with almond crust and cinnamon

A soft and crumbly sweet cousin of our original focaccia. The crispy crust and either almonds or nuts transform the idea of flatbread to a delicious cake bread, very quickly made and eaten just as fast. That's why this is a recipe for a large one.

ONE LARGE OR TWO SMALL CAKE BREADS
8-10 SERVINGS AS DESSERT, E.G. WITH CINNAMON SYRIUP

PREPARATION TIME 100 MINUTES:
1 HOUR OF REST FOR THE DOUGH INCLUDED
PLUS 30–35 MINUTES BAKING TIME

Ingredients:

4 cups (500 g) all-purpose flour
100 g ground almonds
5 g salt
21 g fresth yeast (or 7 g dried yeast)
3 tablespoons vegetable oil
350 ml lukewarm water
6 tablespoons brown sugar

For the crust:

50 g brown sugar
50 g vegan butter or margarine
2 teaspoons ground cinnamon
75 g coarsely chopped almonds

BRUSH WITH MELTED MARGARINE OR VEGAN BUTTER
AND BEST SERVE WARM DIRECTLY FROM THE OVEN

Dissolve yeast and sugar in the lukewarm water and place the bowl in a warm place for 15 minutes.

Take a large bowl and mix flour, ground almonds, oil and salt together thoroughly. Now add the water with the yeast and knead briefly but properly. Form the dough into one or two or more bales.

Now take a big greased baking tray or casserole dishes - we take 3 small baking dishes for lasagne to make this recipe. Put the dough on the tray or into the dishes and remember: It will rise high and needs a little space.

Melt the margarine and spread it on top. Cover generously with cinnamon, sugar and chopped almonds. Leave to rise in the still switched off oven. Remove from oven.

Preheat to 390°F (200°C) and bake for 30 to 35 minutes until golden and delicious.

Tomato Focaccia

Simple but still delicious: Focaccia will accomodate tomato sauce on top or instead of water, sun-dried tomatoes in the dough and as a topping. Combine focaccia with fresh or dried tomato or put an entire shrub on top. Always great.

Sun-dried tomatoes in oil or without can be chopped and kneaded into the dough or simply sprinkled on top of the focaccia.

The standard recipe for focaccia (the first in this book) can be used to make two medium-sized flat breads. Put an entire intact shrub of mini cocktail tomatoes on top before baking. Sprinkled with salt and fresh rosemary they will be an enchanting eyecatcher on a buffet.

Use tomato sauce instead of water when making focaccia and the dough will take on a reddish colour - a nice base for a pretty gardenscape focaccia with vegetables in red, brown and orange on top of the bread.

Recipe Ideas for Party Focaccia

Each focaccia recipe is suitable for toppings with herbs and vegetables, can be filled like a pizza calzone and decorated with ingredients that are put directly into the dough. Some inspiration for parties and guests.

THE PHOTO ON PAGE 22 SHOWS A FOCACCIA WITH FRIED ONIONS IN THE DOUGH AND OLIVES ON TOP

Focaccia topped with freshly caramelized onions that are put on before baking

Focaccia with sun-dried tomato and walnut in the dough and on top

Left: Wholemeal focaccia filled with cheese and topped with slices of tomato
Right: Cauliflower focaccia with fresh sage topping, pizza style.

SEMOLINA FOCACCIA WITH GARLIC IN CHILI OIL AND BLANCHED BRUSSEL SPROUTS

Peach Focaccia with garlic and chili flakes

Fruit on top does not automatically mean sweet focaccia. For this recipe, we kneaded chili pickled garlic into the dough and sprinkled the flatbread with chili flakes - the result is a ravishing contrast and a dance on your tongue.

THE PEACH FOCACCIA WAS BAKED USING THE STANDARD FOCACCIA RECIPE ON PAGE 7

BAKED AT 390°F (200°C) IN THE PREHEATED OVEN 60 MIN REST FOR THE DOUGH 20-25 MIN BAKING TIME

Ingredients:

either 3 ripe peaches in soft pieces
or
3–4 medium ripe peaches in fine slices

chopped garlic marinated in chili oil, crushed and kneaded into the dough

chili flakes and coarse sea-salt, both from the mill

If you like it a litle less hot, leave out the spicy garlic and take fresh thyme instead of chili.
Open to experiments?
Try plum, chili and nutmeg combined or try fresh basil on pineapple slices.

Most focaccia recipes will immediately collect some fans, declaring each new bread variant a favorite one after the other. But spirits are often divided when sweet and spicy are combined.

We recommend to divide the dough to make one traditional focaccia and one with a more exotic topping when baking for guests.

Lemon Focaccia with Herbs

Very pretty focaccia bread, easy to make with all kinds of citrus fruits. Lemon focaccia is gorgeous and complements tapas and antipasti. Fresh lemons can be used as well als pickled salt lemons.

FINELY PEELED LEMON SLICES WITH BLACK OLIVES AND TWIGS OF FRESH THYME

CLASSIC FOCACCIA, BAKE IN THE PREHEATED OVEN FOR 20-25 MINUTES

You don't like the taste of lemon in your bread? Try grapefruit or orange slices, combined with chili and fresh herbs such as basil, rosemary and thyme.

Salt preserved lemons from the oriental supermarket are both milder and more aromatic compared to fresh ones. They are well worth making, but it takes 4 to 6 weeks.

Salt lemons don't need to be peeled and they taste so wonderful with fresh rosemary. But don't take a wholemeal focaccia recipe for this, it's nicer with a lighter flour.

Focaccia Art: Flowers with Herbal Stems

A simple single flower is an elegant start into focaccia gardening. You don't have to bake a big vegetable breadscape to get very pretty results, some leftover veggies will do just fine.

TWO OR THREE VEGETABLE FLOWERS WITH HERBAL STEMS ARE A FAST AND EASY WAY TO START MAKING VERY PRETTY FOCACCIA ART.

Before putting your vegetables on top of the dough we advise you to try and plan your design on a seperate plate. The reason: Even for a focacia that covers the entire baking tray you will only need very few vegetables. To avoid waste, you need to get a feeling for the layout on top of the focaccia bread.,

Radish slices dyed red with beetroot juice. Chives, parsley and rosemary stems on a focaccia flatbread of 10 inches (25 cm) diameter.

Colourful peppers, carrots and herbs with long stems are a good starter setup for flower focaccia.

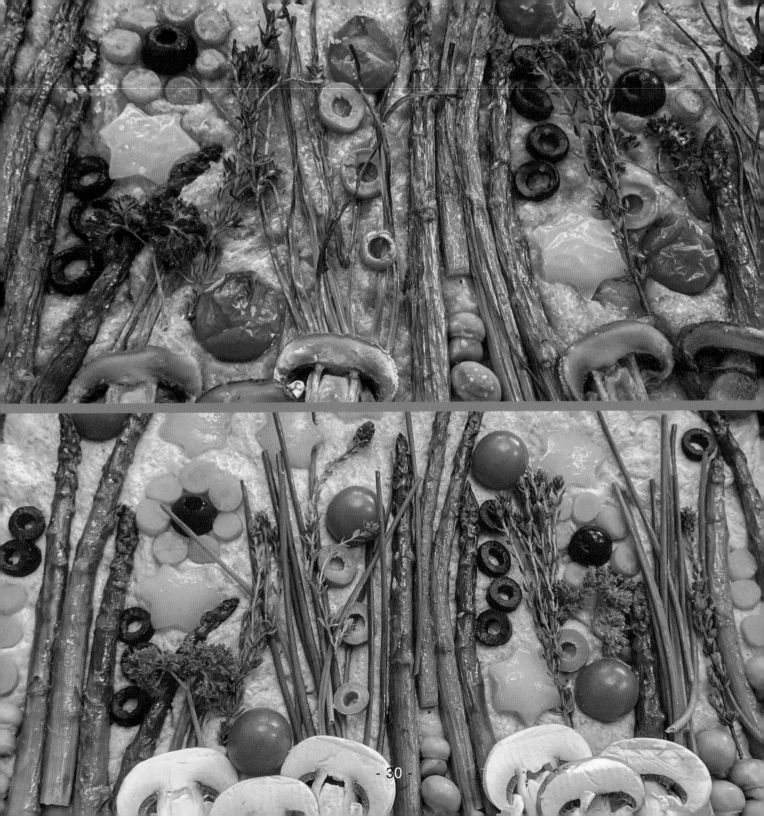

Focaccia Gardenscape – Breadscape Meadows

You don't need many vegetables to make one of the beautiful Focaccia Gardenscapes. Most likely you are going to end up with enough ingredients for a veggie side dish or a salad anyway. Both complement focaccia nicely.

TRADITIONAL FOCACCIA ON A BAKING TRAY OF 12X18 INCHES (30X45 CM) WITH A VEGETABLE GARDENSCAPE

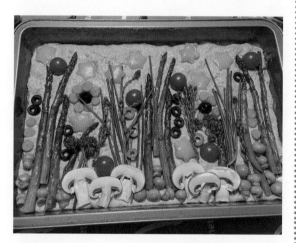

Almost all types of vegetables are suitable for colourful Focaccia Gardens.

Try antipasti and pickled vegetables as well as beans, nuts, mushrooms or lentils.

When putting sliced tomatoes on top, please dab them dry carefully after removing seeds and juices.

Mushrooms and asparagus are best when briefly marinated in oil and lemon juice. Harder vegetables should be blanched not only to be soft enough, but also for color.

YOU ONLY NEED THIS MANY INGREDIENTS IF YOU PUT YOUR FAMILY ON FOCACCIA DIET TO MAKE A COOKBOOK.

To get the best results for your herbs in a focaccia garden, let them marinate for an hour in lemon water before putting them on the bread. Also make sure they are put on last, after brushing with oil and sprinkling with salt.

Mandala Focaccia as party food highlight

Need to use up all the leftovers from making salad and buffet dishes? #mandalafocaccia spirals and patterns look very pretty and are really easy to make, even for smaller children.

Ingredients for the big mandala:
frozen green peas
canned chick peas
canned corn
sliced red onions
chopped red pepper
black olives in slices
frozen pumpkin cubes

Leftover dough from making a bigger gardenscape will probably be enough to make a nice little #mandalafocaccia.

If you want the pattern to stick in place when baking, you have to make sure the focaccia is pushed down a little to be flat - the bigger, the flatter.

In the photo, from the inside out: black olive, carrot slices, green olive slices, sliced pepper in two colours, black olives in slices. The bread has a diameter of approximately 8 inches (20 cm).

Fabulous Magnificence: Fairytale Focaccia

Colourful upgrade for Gardenscapes: Fairytale Focaccia, dyed breadscapes meant to be eyecatchers on every buffet. So far we have only found our own #fairytalefocaccia, but we are looking forward to many more from now on!

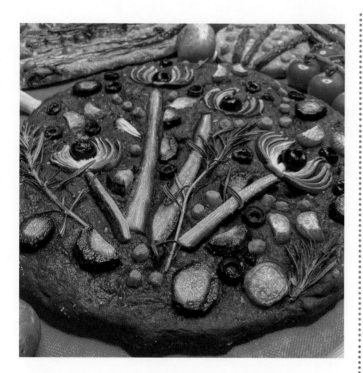

Topping for our red Fairytale Focaccia:

- 1 red onion, sliced lengthwise to make petals
- 2 thick purple carrots in slices all over the bread plus halves of long stripes as stems
- 3 small orange carrots in delicate slices
- 4–5 pieces of radish, sliced in half as butterfly
- 2 large black olives, in halves / 4 pieces
- 1 fistful of black olive slices
- whole rosemary twigs as undergrowth
- some virgin olive oil
- coarse sea-salt
- lots of beetroot powder spice kneaded into the dough

Fairytale Focaccia can be pink or purple, if you knead beetroot powder into the dough - you can create many pretty shades. Try turmeric for yellow, pureed baby spinach (lots of it) for green or buy some organic blue food paint.

More Tips for the Making of Focaccia Art

Focaccia Gardenscape, like all focaccia recipe, taste best warm and fresh from the oven. Are you planning to give your Foccacia Art away or take it to a party, please keep this in mind when planning your overall schedule.

THE PICTURE SHOWS A FOCACCIA WITH SALT LEMONS AND ROSEMARY AMONG THE VEGETABLES NECESSARY FOR THE RED FAIRYTALE FOCACCIA FROM PAGE 34.

It has proved to be a good idea to place the largest parts like stems first. Add the bottom of the flower picture (e.g. mushrooms) before putting oil and salt on top. Marinate the herbs in lemon juice and put on last.

It does not matter whether you put the bread on a tray or use a baking dish. Brush the underground with oil and sprinkle with semolina. Every Focaccia, even those filled with veggie art, are brushed with a little more oil and sprinkled with salt, before the herbs are put on top and the bread into the preheated oven.

OUR EXPERIENCE IN WRITING THIS COOKBOOK HAS SHOWN: THE MOST IMPORTANT INGREDIENT IN FAIRYTALE FOCACCIA IS JOY.

Different Kinds of Flour (all-purpose will do)

The quality of the flour you are using determines how tasty a bread or cake are going to be. If you are not a regular baker, you might not even realize how many different types of flour exist and what they are meant for.

FOCACCIA BEFORE GETTING HER TOPPING AND BEING BRUSHED WITH OIL AND SPRINKLED WITH SALT.

The best flour for a focaccia is Italian pizza flour type OO, mixed with a little durum wheat semolina (which is also sprinkled on the oiled baking sheet)...

Sounds simple? This is complicated by the fact that in Italy there are many types of flour of OO, namely different ones for pasta, pizza and bread - but not even the pizza flour can be found everywhere abroad.

Fortunately, a nice focaccia made with love and patience will accept almost every kind of flour.

The German System: The type numbers on the different flours indicate the mineral content of the flour in milligrams to one hundred grams (mg / 100 g). The lower the number, the more refined and lighter the flour.

Type 405 wheat flour therefore contains 405 milligrams of minerals per 100 grams. To determine the content, 100 g of flour are burned at 900 ° C. What remains is the non-combustible mineral content, the amount of which determines the type number.

International bakers: If you can't get high-gluten pizza flour, bread flour or all-purpose flour will do just fine.

#Foodblog
Family-Recipes
COOKING FOR GUESTS
veganizing
#vegan
#germanBlog
#mealprep

WWW.PLANET-ALLTAG.DE #foodie
planet-alltag.de/newsletter

© 2020 Carola Heine
Fairytale Focaccia
ISBN: 978-3-948033-19-4

1. Edition

Author and Publisher:
Carola Heine
Rather Kirchplatz 2a
DE-40472 Düsseldorf Germany
kontakt@one-trick-pony.de
www.planet-alltag.de/english

Proofreading: Oliver Heine-Bonkowski
Cover: Carola Heine
Design: Carola Heine with canva.com

E-Book Platform and Print
KDP von Amazon Media EU S.à r.l.
38 Avenue John F. Kennedy -L-1855 Luxembourg
*

Planet Alltag

Follow us on instagram or pinterest for bilingual posts :-)

instagram:
@fabulous.focaccia

planet-alltag.de

Printed in Great Britain
by Amazon

26462016R00023